DATE DUE			

WILMA RUDOLPH

The African-American Biographies Series

—African-American Biographies—

WILMA RUDOLPH

The Greatest Woman Sprinter in History

Series Consultant:
Dr. Russell L. Adams, Chairman
Department of Afro-American Studies, Howard University

Anne Schraff

Enslow Publishers, Inc.

40 Industrial Road	PO Box 38
Box 398	Aldershot
Berkeley Heights, NJ 07922	Hants GU12 6BP
USA	UK

http://www.enslow.com

Library of Congress Cataloging-in-Publication Data

Schraff, Anne E.
  Wilma Rudolph : the greatest woman sprinter in history / Anne Schraff.
      p. cm. — (African-American Biographies)
  Summary: Profiles Wilma Rudolph, who overcame childhood polio to become an
Olympic medal-winning runner.
  Includes bibliographical references and index.
  ISBN 0-7660-2291-9 (hardcover)
  1. Rudolph, Wilma, 1940– —Juvenile literature. 2. Runners (Sports)—United
States—Biography—Juvenile literature. 3. Women runners—United States—
Biography—Juvenile literature. [1. Rudolph, Wilma, 1940– 2. Track and field
athletes. 3. African Americans—Biography. 4. Women—Biography.]
  I. Title. II. Series.
  GV1061.15.R83S35 2004
  796.42'092—dc22
                                            2003014971

Printed in the United States of America

10 9 8 7 6 5 4 3 2 1

To Our Readers:
We have done our best to make sure all Internet Addresses in this book were active and
appropriate when we went to press. However, the author and the publisher have no control over and assume no liability for the material available on those Internet sites or on
other Web sites they may link to. Any comments or suggestions can be sent by e-mail to
comments@enslow.com or to the address on the back cover.

Every effort has been made to locate all copyright holders of material used in this book.
If any errors or omissions have occurred, corrections will be made in future editions of
this book.

Illustration Credits: AP/Madison Square Garden, p. 63; AP/Wide World
Photos, pp. 17, 33, 48, 52, 80, 85, 97; Clinton Presidential Materials Project,
pp. 90, 91; clipart.com, p. 24; Courtesy of Special Collections and Archives,
Tennessee State University, p. 39; Library of Congress, pp. 6, 30, 45, 49, 59,
66, 69, 79.

Cover Illustration: AP/Wide World Photos

Contents

Wilma Rudolph

1

THE FEELING OF FREEDOM

ixteen-year-old Wilma Rudolph, a lanky girl from Tennessee, was taking part in her first Olympics. It was October 1956, and it seemed nothing short of a miracle that she was here at all.

Only four years earlier, Wilma was wearing a heavy steel leg brace and orthopedic shoes. She needed these to help her walk after a childhood of illness and disability. She had longed to join the other children at play and took to running when she was freed of the brace. She later said, "I loved the feeling of freedom in running, the fresh air, the feeling that the only person I'm really competing with is me."[1]

After years of determination and hard work, Wilma had made it to the Olympics in Melbourne, Australia. A short time earlier, Wilma had not even known what the Olympics were. But now she knew she would be competing against athletes from all over the world. The Olympics were very important. Everybody back in Wilma's hometown of Clarksville, Tennessee, would be watching to see how well she did.

Wilma hoped to run in the 200-meter dash, but first she had to qualify. She finished third in the qualifying heat (the race to decide who runs in the official race). Wilma had not run fast enough to compete for the medal.

"I felt terrible after," Wilma said later. She could not eat or sleep. "I felt as if I had let down everybody back home and the whole United States of America."[2] In Melbourne, far from home, the teenager felt like a failure, but she would get one more chance to win a medal. Wilma qualified to run in the 400-meter relay race with three other girls.

On the day of the relay race, Wilma was nervous. If she lost here, she would go back to Clarksville without a medal. Mae Faggs ran the first leg of the relay race, and she got the American team off to a good start. Margaret Matthews ran the second leg and kept the momentum going. It was Wilma's turn next. She grabbed the baton and ran the third leg of the race, passing two girls from competing teams. Then she passed the baton to Isabelle Daniels, who ran the last leg. The American runners did not win the close race, but they still performed well. They came in third and were awarded the bronze medal.

Wilma and her teammates stood on the victory stand to receive their bronze medals. Wilma was disappointed she had not been able to run the 200-meter race, but she said later, "A bronze medal still isn't all that bad for a high school kid from Tennessee."[3]

It was not all that bad indeed. To win a medal at the Olympics is a great achievement. As Wilma later said, "Most people don't realize that you work a lifetime to run 9-10-11 seconds. No matter how many years you train to try to become the best, at that point anybody in the race has the same chance."[4]

2

CHILDHOOD STRUGGLE

ilma Glodean Rudolph was born on June 23, 1940, in tiny St. Bethlehem, Tennessee, a community of farms about fifty miles southeast of Nashville. Wilma arrived two months early, after her mother fell at home. The underweight baby had problems eating because she was so small.

Wilma's mother, Blanche Rudolph, worked as a maid in the homes of rich white people six days a week. Blanche could read and write, unlike her husband. When there were big decisions to be made in the family, she read the necessary documents aloud, and he made the decisions. She was a resourceful woman who collected flour sacks with printed patterns on them to make clothing for her children. Sometimes she earned more money working as a cook at a café for white people, bringing home extra food for her own family.

Though Blanche Rudolph had a very hard life, she did not complain. Wilma later recalled, "I never once saw my mother cry."[1] A deeply religious Baptist, Blanche Rudolph was quiet. "So proud, so strong, so religious," her daughter said.[2] Wilma often went to her mother and gave her a hug and a kiss. Though there was not much conversation between Wilma and her mother, Wilma said, "We both knew there was love there."[3]

Edward Rudolph, Wilma's father, was a strict disciplinarian. He told his children that if they did not go to church on Sunday, they could not do anything else that day. He worked as a railroad porter, a high-status job for black men at the time. Porters were well-respected members of the black community. They belonged to the Brotherhood of Sleeping Car Porters, once the most powerful black union in U.S. history. Edward Rudolph also earned extra money painting houses and cutting firewood. He stressed to his children that school was very important. Wilma found it was easier to talk to her father than to her mother, and she felt very close to him.[4]

Edward Rudolph was the father of eleven children

from a previous marriage. He and Blanche then went on to have eight more children together. Wilma was their fifth child. The older eleven were already out of the house and on their own during Wilma's childhood.

Shortly after Wilma's birth, the family moved to Clarksville, the fifth largest city in Tennessee. The family had a combined income of $2,500 a year—not a lot of money for such a large family. At that time, the average American worker earned about $2,000 annually.

The Rudolph home was a large wood-frame house with no electricity. There was a wood-burning stove in the kitchen and fireplaces in various rooms for heat. Kerosene lamps and sometimes candles provided light. The black people of Clarksville all lived in similar houses, and there was constant fear of fire from an overturned kerosene lamp. There was no indoor plumbing. The family used an outhouse. Wilma was aware at an early age that white people lived in better houses with electricity and indoor plumbing. She thought, "There's something not right about this."[5]

Clarksville was a segregated community, which meant that blacks and whites were taught in separate schools, used separate drinking fountains and rest rooms, and had to sit in the back seats of buses. With almost everything they did, blacks were reminded that they had a lower status than whites.

When Wilma was about four years old, she became very sick with double pneumonia (a serious lung disease) and scarlet fever (a once widespread childhood disease causing a bright red rash). Wilma's mother treated her with home remedies like hot toddies, which are hot drinks made with sugar, liquor, and herbs. She also sweat the child, piling blankets on Wilma in an effort to sweat out the poisons of the illness in her body.[6] The Rudolphs had no money to spare for doctors, so they relied on these methods to see their children through many illnesses. But Wilma was not like the other children. As she recovered from the fever, her mother noticed her left leg was crooked and her foot turned inward. The child had trouble walking.

Blanche Rudolph took Wilma to Doctor Coleman, the only black doctor in Clarksville. He said that while she was weakened by the other disease, Wilma had apparently contracted polio. This was a very serious disease that killed and paralyzed thousands of children in the years before a vaccine was developed by Dr. Jonas Salk in 1954. Dr. Coleman told Wilma's mother that Wilma might not walk again, but Wilma said, "My mother told me I would, so I believed my mother."[7]

There was no hospital in Clarksville that would treat blacks, so black people needing medical help had to travel about fifty miles into Nashville to Meharry Medical College. Wilma's mother and her small daughter took the bus for the long journey.

There were specialists at Meharry as well as exercise equipment and whirlpools used to strengthen the muscles of paralyzed patients. After examining Wilma, the doctors set up a therapy plan. She would go to the hospital twice a week. "They were forever pulling, turning, twisting, lifting that leg," Wilma said later.[8] Her leg was pulled up into the air in traction, a method of treating damaged limbs. All the time this was going on, Wilma's mother sat by her side reading stories to her. Once Wilma's leg was lowered, it was plunged into hot water. This treatment was very painful, but Wilma endured it, hoping her leg would get better.

It was hard for Wilma's mother to go to Nashville twice a week. She had other children in the family to care for, and she forfeited her pay whenever she took time off from work. If she did not work, she did not get paid.

The physical therapists at Meharry taught Blanche Rudolph how to massage Wilma's leg at home. Four times every day, Wilma's mother, her older sisters, or her brothers would give her a treatment. Wilma credited her recovery to her family's loving care. "With all the love and care my family gave me, I couldn't help but get better," she said.[9]

Still, the road to recovery was long and hard. Wilma's leg was fitted with a steel brace. It hooked onto her leg just above the knee and went all the way down to connect with her shoe. The brace was designed to keep her leg from going sideways. She had to put it on when she got up in the morning, and she could not take it off until bedtime. "It looked so terrible," Wilma said later.[10] She envied the other little girls in their pretty, dainty shoes. She always had to wear brown lace-up shoes with her brace.

"The brace," Wilma said, "always reminded me something was wrong with me."[11] She knew she needed the brace, but still she hated it. Sometimes when both her parents were out of the house, she would remove the brace and try walking without it. She posted her brothers and sisters at the doors to watch for the return of their parents. As they approached, she would quickly get back into her brace.[12]

During those years, Wilma spent a lot of time in bed or in a chair. Her family tried to keep her spirits up. Her brothers and sisters were very good about playing with her inside because she could not go outside. Still, it seemed to Wilma that she was constantly bedridden. At night, at family prayers, Wilma always said, "I pray this leg gets better and I can be healthy like everybody else."[13]

Wilma spent a lot of time daydreaming as her sisters and brothers went off to school and left her behind. She sometimes imagined herself living in a large white house on a hill, being married with kids.[14]

Since Wilma could not go to school, a tutor came by to teach her reading, writing, and arithmetic. Her brothers and sisters also helped teach her. Wilma struggled to keep up her hopes of being able to walk, but sometimes she grew discouraged. She would study her skinny leg and not see any improvement. She said later she would get "mad about it all."[15] But she did not grow bitter. Instead she grew stubbornly determined, as she said, to "beat these illnesses no matter what."[16]

Dr. Coleman came frequently to the Rudolph house to check on Wilma. She thought he was "a beautiful man," adding that he was "so kind and nice."[17] He assured the little girl that everything would turn out all right and urged her to keep on fighting.

In spite of her struggles with poor health, Wilma had many happy times during her childhood too. Although the family had little money, she said they had "everything else, especially love."[18] There was no money for the movies and the family took no newspaper, but they had a small radio and a Victrola record player for playing music. Wilma especially enjoyed the blues singing of Billie Holiday.

The two best times for Wilma were Christmas and the annual Clarksville County Fair. Christmas was always wonderful because relatives brought gifts for the children. The fair was exciting because the black children of the town would sit in the tall grass and watch all the colorful sights and sounds as gaily decorated horses and wagons would arrive.

Because of her leg, Wilma missed kindergarten and first grade, but when she was seven years old she was

Wilma, age six, with her older sister Yvonne.

able to attend Cobb Elementary School, where her brothers and sisters went. Like all black schools, Cobb did not have as many books as the white schools, but the teachers were good. They stressed reading and writing, and Wilma was very glad to be there. She was so excited to be one of the kids in school instead of that sickly little girl sitting at home. "I needed to belong and I finally did," she said later.[19]

Wilma's first teacher was Mrs. Allison, a kind and generous person who became a role model for Wilma. She encouraged Wilma to join the Brownies, a Scout group for girls in second and third grades. When Wilma could not afford the Brownie uniform, Mrs. Allison said it was fine if she just wore brown shoes and socks. Wilma was able to participate in all the Brownie activities. Mrs. Allison built up Wilma's self-confidence.

In fourth grade, Wilma had a very different experience. Her teacher, Mrs. Hoskins, had the reputation of being the "toughest teacher in the whole school."[20] Wilma got her first spanking from Mrs. Hoskins, but still Wilma admired her because she did not play favorites. She was fair to everyone. Mrs. Hoskins drilled a can-do spirit into Wilma. She said, "Don't dream about it. Wilma, I want you to do it."[21] Wilma would remember that advice for the rest of her life. It would shape her attitude in everything she did.

In a combination fifth-and-sixth grade, Wilma had a male teacher. She did not like him because he ignored the fifth-graders and preferred to teach the older children. One day he tried to give Wilma a strapping across her hand for a minor misdeed. She refused to walk up to the front of the room to be punished. When the teacher threatened to send her to the principal, Wilma stood her ground. She believed she was being unjustly punished. Finally, the teacher backed down. For Wilma, the incident became a turning point in her life. "I had stood up for my rights," she said later, "and won."[22]

Wilma was going to school, but she still could not join the children in their outdoor games. Because she was different, she was teased and ridiculed by some children. Wilma grew more determined every day to be rid of the cumbersome leg brace.

Sometimes Wilma would play basketball with her older brothers. It was an easy game for her because she could stand in one place and shoot the ball into the basket. Once in a while, she removed her brace and brown lace-up shoes and played barefoot.

At the age of nine, Wilma was able to take off the brace, put on regular shoes, and walk several steps. That encouraged her. But she still had to wear the brown shoes most of the time. Her brothers and sisters continued to encourage her and play games with her.

Finally, in 1952, the lanky twelve-year-old was walking in regular shoes. At last she could take part in the sports she loved so much. She had spent so many years wistfully watching other children at play and at sports, and now she was ready to make up for lost time. She felt like someone freed from prison. She began to run and jump. She challenged every boy in the neighborhood to footraces and usually won.[23] That steel brace had been no match for Wilma's steely resolve.

3

A Star Athlete Is Born

 or many long years, Wilma Rudolph sat on the sidelines watching other young people play basketball. She had hoped that one day she could really join in, but she was not idling away her time. She was learning a lot about the game, about strategies and rules. So when she was freed of her braces and her heavy brown shoes, she hit the courts running. She was ready.

Wilma played basketball with her brothers and sisters, but she was eager to play on a real school team. She was counting on playing for Burt High School, where she was starting seventh grade.

The newly built Burt High School in Clarksville, Tennessee, enrolled students in grades seven through twelve. The students were proud of their handsome school. "It gave all the kids something to look forward to each day," Wilma said.[1] Many of the black schools in the segregated South were in poor repair in the 1950s. Burt High School was a bright, shiny exception to the rule.

Burt High School had a solid basketball team, and Wilma was already almost six feet tall. She was agile and strong. Her hopes were high.

There was some prejudice at the time against girls getting seriously involved in sports. Many people believed that sports were just for boys. They looked at sports as unfeminine. Wilma often heard that a woman "couldn't be a lady and a good athlete at the same time."[2] Wilma did not believe this. She loved sports, and when the game was over she enjoyed dressing up and looking beautiful. She ignored the prejudices and went all out in sports.[3]

As much as Wilma wanted to play basketball, she could not persuade the coach, Clinton Gray, to take her on the team. Wilma's mother was not too excited about her daughter playing basketball, either. She was afraid that Wilma would be injured, and all those years of therapy would have been for nothing. But Wilma's father knew how badly she wanted to play, and he supported her.

Coach Gray finally agreed to give Wilma private lessons for ten minutes a day in the morning. When he thought she was good enough to hold her own with the more experienced players, he tried her out. Wilma joined the team, but after a few games she was cut. Gray did not think the freshman was yet good enough for the Burt team. But he did want Wilma's older sister, Yvonne, to play. When Edward Rudolph, Wilma's father, found out about this, he intervened on Wilma's behalf. He told Coach Gray he could have Yvonne on his team only if he took Wilma, too. So, in her sophomore year, Wilma was back on the team.

At first Wilma spent most of her time sitting on the bench. Still, she made the most of bench time watching the other girls and studying their moves and strategies. She was sure that when she finally got her chance to play, she would be great. Wilma also enjoyed other benefits of being on the team: When the Burt team played away from home, Wilma got the chance to travel to other towns.

In a game near the end of the season, when the Burt team was well behind in points, Coach Gray gave Wilma a chance. But with only seconds to play, Wilma panicked. While she was dribbling the ball, she was so nervous that she fell at Coach Gray's feet. He told her that she reminded him of a mosquito, always in his way. From that encounter, Wilma got a new nickname: Skeeter.

Wilma spent years watching other kids play basketball and studying their moves.

At last Wilma got the chance to join the effort in a winning game. When another girl threw her the ball, she heard a chorus of yells urging her to shoot. To her delight, she made the basket and helped the team to a victory.

Little by little, Wilma got more playing time. She became so good that Coach Gray put her in the starting lineup. Wilma quickly became a favorite with the spectators. Now six feet tall and graceful, Wilma scored 803 points in twenty-five games, a record in the state of Tennessee for girls' basketball.

A crucial big game was the Middle East Tennessee Conference game. Wilma was the starting guard. She scored 10 points to help her team gain a spot in the Tennessee High School Girls' Championship. Wilma was riding high until she participated in the losing game that knocked Burt out of the regional finals. She blamed herself for the loss. Still, out of the game came a new opportunity that Wilma had never dreamed of.

One of the referees in the championship game was Ed Temple, the women's track coach at Tennessee State Agricultural and Industrial University (known as Tennessee A & I, and later renamed Tennessee State University) in Nashville, Tennessee. He coached the Tigerbelles, a powerful women's track team with a legendary record for creating champions.

Temple had previously been the referee for games in which Wilma played. He had not been impressed. One time he even called Wilma over and told her she was too lazy to jump.[4] Then he told Coach Gray to put a mark up on a wall and make Wilma jump at it twenty or thirty times a day until she hit it. Coach Gray took his advice, and Wilma began jumping higher and higher to hit the target. Wilma did not mind Ed Temple's comment because, as she said, he was "always fair" in the games.[5] She also liked the fact that he called the players by name instead of number.

But in the championship game, Ed Temple saw a Wilma Rudolph he had not seen before. "The first time I set eyes on Wilma was when she was playing basketball," he said.[6] But suddenly he was seeing her as a possible champion in another sport: Looking at Wilma, he saw a natural sprinter.

Wilma was no stranger to running. When she had gotten rid of her brace and her lace-up shoes, she had begun running for fun. Now, between practicing and playing basketball, she was taking part in Burt High School's very informal track program. The girls on the track team did not even have a track on which to practice, so they ran through the school halls in bad weather and over fields in good weather. They played against other schools, but the games were so informal that nobody even kept records.

Wilma enjoyed running. She had been bedridden for so long that she was all the more delighted by the sensation of racing over hill and dale. "I never forgot all the years when I was a little girl," she said later, "and not able to be involved. When I ran I felt like a butterfly. That feeling was always there."[7]

Ed Temple encouraged Coach Gray to start a real track team at Burt High School. He wanted Wilma and the other girls to get the experience they would need for college competition. In 1956, when Wilma was sixteen, she took part in the first official women's track meet in Alabama. The Amateur Athletic Union (AAU) invited young women from all over the South to compete in races at Tuskegee University in Tuskegee, Alabama.

Wilma had never seen a college campus before. She was excited not only about the races, but also about being out of her immediate area for the first time in her life. Except for a few away games with her basketball team in neighboring towns, Wilma had never gone far from home. To add to the excitement, on the weekend there were going to be dances. All the girls, including Wilma, had brought their best dress.

The night before the races, Wilma was nervous. But by the time she got to the track the next day, she felt confident. She looked the other competitors over and assured herself, "I could wipe them out because, after all, I had won every single race I had ever been in up to that point."[8]

But the meet at Tuskegee was to be a rude awakening for the lanky young athlete. She was in way over her head. The other competitors had a lot more experience on real track teams, and Wilma did not win a single race.

Wilma learned a lot from the defeat at Tuskegee. She said it taught her that a person cannot win "on natural ability alone, and there was more to track than just running fast."[9] But still, for many weeks after Tuskegee, Wilma's confidence was shattered.[10]

When she got home, she ran every day, even cutting classes at Burt High to run. She ran herself ragged, determined that the following year she would return to Tuskegee and beat everyone.

In spite of Wilma's poor showing at Tuskegee,

Coach Temple was not discouraged with her. He knew her lack of success was the result of inexperience. In May 1956, Temple came to visit Wilma's parents to tell them about a summer program to train promising female high school runners. He assured Wilma's parents that their daughter would be well chaperoned and watched over by a house mother in the dormitories. The girls would not be allowed to ride in cars or go to nightclubs. It was lights-out every night at nine.

The summer program at Tennessee A & I was a great opportunity for Wilma. All expenses were paid, and Coach Temple promised to pick Wilma up at her home in Clarksville and drive her to the university.

Wilma settled in her room at Wilson Hall and was issued two T-shirts, shorts, a sweatsuit, and shoes. The first morning, Wilma was up at six with the other girls and then ran until eight. After breakfast, Wilma ran another six miles, and after lunch still another six miles. The girls in the program ran twenty miles every day. On Sunday there was church, the movies, and time to read or just rest.

Wilma ran cross-country over hills and farmlands. The purpose was to build endurance. She learned how to improve her performance by holding her hands a certain way. When a runner forms a tight fist, her entire body tenses up. Wilma learned to run with open hands. She learned to run leaning forward. Some of the girls were leaning backward as they ran. By leaning forward or into the race, speed improves. Wilma learned how to breathe properly, taking long, deep breaths.

Wilma had problems with her starts. She lacked speed coming out of the starting blocks. It took her longer to gain speed because of that. At Nashville she learned to accept her problem with starts and to compensate for them by using her strong points.

Wilma learned to perfect her skill in relay teams. One of the most difficult actions in a relay race is passing the baton from one runner to the next. Wilma developed the ability to cut her stride just enough to smoothly grasp the baton, and to pass it.

In August 1956, the big AAU meet was being held in Philadelphia, Pennsylvania. It was Wilma's first trip north, and she was impressed by the historic city. She was completely awed when she walked into the large Franklin Field stadium. She said that she "nearly fainted," and she "felt like a midget."[11]

Wilma was facing serious competition and an important test. How much had she learned in her summer at Nashville? Competing with far more experienced runners, Wilma won the 75- and 100-yard dashes, and she anchored the winning relay team. The anchor in a relay team is the runner who runs the last—and most important—leg of the race.

Wilma Rudolph had won her first important races. She had proved to herself that she was the real thing.

After her triumph, Wilma got an unexpected treat

Wilma was thrilled to meet Jackie Robinson. She called him her "first black hero."

when she met the legendary baseball player Jackie Robinson. Robinson, the first black player in the major leagues, had won the respect of the nation when he overcame bigoted taunts and insults with grace and style. He opened major league baseball to all the black players who came after him.

Wilma posed for photographs with Robinson, who told her, "I really like your style of running and I really think you have a lot of potential."[12] Wilma was deeply touched by the friendliness and graciousness of the famous man toward a teenager from Clarksville, Tennessee. "Jackie Robinson after that day was my first black hero," she said.[13]

Wilma Rudolph was just sixteen years old, and an almost unimaginable prospect was opening up for her. Coach Temple told her that he wanted her to compete in the 1956 Olympics in Melbourne, Australia.

In just two weeks, the Olympic trials would be held in Seattle, Washington. Wilma agreed, and soon she and several other girls were driving toward Seattle, with Coach Temple at the wheel.

In the 200-meter trial heat, Wilma Rudolph qualified for the Olympics. She would be the youngest member of the United States Olympic Team.

After a two-week training camp prior to leaving for Australia, Wilma and her teammates boarded a plane bound for Melbourne. Very soon the whole world would watch Wilma run.

4

THE TIGERBELLE

hough still a high school junior, Wilma Rudolph had gone to the Olympic Games in Melbourne, Australia, and won a bronze medal in the 400-meter relay race. Wilma Rudolph and her three teammates ran a good race and gained a strong third-place finish. All four girls stood on the victory stand, proudly wearing their bronze medals.

Melbourne had been an exciting experience for Wilma. For the first time in her life people were asking for her autograph. Sometimes she stood for two hours signing autographs for fans. It was quite a boost to her self-esteem. The girl from Clarksville, Tennessee, had

The runners of the American women's track team proudly show their bronze medals: from left, Margaret Matthews, Wilma Rudolph, Mae Faggs, and Isabelle Daniels.

been welcomed to Hawaii with her fellow Olympians by hula dancers who gave them leis. Wilma had mingled with athletes from all over the world. The world was suddenly a much bigger place for Wilma Rudolph.

When Wilma returned home, she was no longer just a speedy little local track star. At Burt High School, Wilma was greeted by a huge banner reading WELCOME HOME, WILMA.[1] The students passed her bronze medal around from hand to hand to see it close up. When Wilma finally got the medal back, there were smudges all over it. She tried to shine the smudges off, but then she realized that bronze does not take a shine. She decided that her next medal would be gold.[2]

Life settled down pretty quickly for Wilma. She continued playing basketball and running on the high school track team. The prom was coming up and Wilma had a boyfriend, Robert Eldridge. They had known each other since grade school. He had been a lively little boy back then, and he liked Wilma enough to tease her. She would pretend to be annoyed, but she liked him. When they started high school, a romantic relationship began.

Robert was a star football and basketball player at Burt High. Wilma was an Olympian. They made a striking pair on the high school social scene. Robert asked Wilma to the prom and she accepted. Her family did not have the money to buy her a prom dress, so she borrowed a formal blue dress from a friend. Robert bought Wilma a white orchid corsage and picked her up in his father's brand-new blue Ford.

After the prom, celebrations continued at a club in Hopkinsville, Kentucky. The club served teenagers alcohol, something they could not get in Clarksville. Although the party got rowdy before morning, Wilma and Robert got safely home. Sadly, one of Wilma's best friends, Nancy Bowen, was not so fortunate.

Nancy Bowen was riding in a car with a boy she did not know well. After leaving the club, he began drag racing at ninety miles an hour. He lost control of the car and struck a concrete bridge support. He and Nancy, who was seated beside him, were killed instantly.

When Wilma learned of Nancy's death in the morning, she was deeply shaken. It was the first time someone close to her had died. "I was an emotional wreck for weeks," she said later. In fact, the terrible accident cast a shadow over Wilma's memories of prom night. The sadness never left her. Years later she said, "To this day I hear the word 'prom' and feel bad."[3] As Wilma began her senior year at Burt High School, her romance with Robert grew more serious. She wore Robert's football jacket at school. They were together every chance they got. "He was always so neat and clean," Wilma said later. "He always dressed better than anybody else, and he wore these cute glasses."[4]

Wilma's parents were very religious and proper, and they expected their children to behave the same way. Edward Rudolph took great pride in his sons who served with bravery in World War II. One was in the Army and the other was in the Air Force, and when they came home they would tell the family stirring stories of their war experiences. So when, at age seventeen, Wilma learned that she was pregnant, she dreaded the thought of telling her parents.

Teachers at Burt High School noticed changes in Wilma, and she finally confided to her older sister Yvonne. Yvonne gave their mother the news, and their mother told their father. Their mother assured Wilma that she would "stick with me, no matter what," Wilma said.[5] Wilma's father blamed Robert for what happened, and he ordered his daughter not to see the boy anymore. Then Edward Rudolph said to Wilma that she need not worry, because "everybody makes mistakes."[6] Wilma was relieved that her family would be supporting her in the difficult time ahead.

Ed Temple had never before allowed a girl who had a baby to participate in the track-and-field program at Tennessee A & I State University, but he told Wilma he would make an exception. After the baby was born, she could become a Tigerbelle.

When Wilma graduated from high school in May 1958, she was seven months pregnant. After her daughter, Yolanda, was born in July, there was a serious problem over who would care for the child. Wilma was scheduled to enter college in September, and she could not do that if she was caring for an infant.

The family discussed having Wilma's parents care for the baby, but Wilma's father was quite ill at the time, making that impossible. Since he was not working, Wilma's mother had to work extra hard to support the family. There were two younger children at home at the time. Wilma's sister Yvonne, who lived in St. Louis with her own young son, finally offered to take Yolanda.

Robert Eldridge wanted to marry Wilma and start their family life together, but Wilma's father forbade any contact between the two young people. Wilma also had dreams of competing in the 1960 Olympics. She would need to do a lot of practicing to make that happen. She could not seriously consider marriage at this time.

One night, right before she left for college, Wilma was in her bedroom with baby Yolanda. She heard a rap on the window. It was Robert. He had not yet seen his new daughter. Wilma opened the window and held Yolanda up to her father. Then Robert went home. He would have very little contact with Yolanda for the next five years.

In September 1958, Yolanda began living in St. Louis with her aunt Yvonne, and Wilma Rudolph became a freshman at Tennessee A & I. To support her college education, Wilma was enrolled in a special work program that Coach Temple had arranged for his athletes. Wilma and the other athletes in the program worked two hours a day, five days a week, at various jobs, cleaning dormitories and serving in the cafeteria. Wilma was majoring in elementary education and psychology.

In high school, Wilma had often allowed her grades to slip a little to make time for her athletic interests. But she could not do that in college. Coach Temple demanded that his athletes make good grades. He wanted them to have something that would see them through life. He knew that none of them, even the superb athletes, would make serious money from their sports achievements.

Wilma had to study hard to maintain the B average she needed to stay in college and be part of the athletic program. Wilma did not see Yolanda from September until December of that year, and she was growing very lonesome for her daughter. But she had become a member of the famed Tennessee track team, the Tigerbelles, and that consumed most of her time.

The Tigerbelles were an amazing group. The women students who belonged to the Tigerbelles had come from all over the country, drawn by the reputation of Coach Ed Temple. Forty women Olympians had started out as Tigerbelles. The three who shared Wilma Rudolph's bronze medal in the 1956 Olympics— Isabelle Daniels, Mae Faggs Starr, and Margaret Matthews—were all Tigerbelles, as was Barbara Jones, who won an Olympic gold medal in 1952.

Sometimes Wilma was intimidated by the high quality of the competition in races at Tennessee A & I. She worked on her breathing techniques, muscle conditioning, and attitude. Slowly, Wilma was able to compete with the best without fear. "It seemed as if I wasn't afraid to challenge anybody anywhere," she said later. "Whatever fears I had, fears of offending somebody else by beating them—all those fears vanished."[7]

To qualify for the 1960 Olympics in Rome, runners went to the national AAU meet in Corpus Christi, Texas. The best women were then invited to the Olympic trials two weeks later at Texas Christian University.

Ed Temple was one of the finest track coaches of his time.

Wilma's memories of the Corpus Christi meet were darkened by an incident on a bus. The bus was full of black and white athletes, all sitting together. When the white bus driver noticed this, he walked off the bus and the athletes had to wait until a bus driver could be found to drive an integrated bus. It was surely not the first experience Wilma had with this kind of racism. When traveling through the segregated South with the Tigerbelles, Ed Temple and his black athletes could not stop to eat at most restaurants, nor could they stay overnight in hotels. Coach Temple's wife, Charlie B., made lunch for the girls and put it in brown sacks for the trips. Often the athletes slept in the cars they came in, getting ready for the track meets in a makeshift fashion. Despite these obstacles, they won most of the time.

Wilma did very well at Corpus Christi and then went to Texas Christian for the Olympic trials. While running the 200-meter race, Wilma ran a 22.9, the fastest 200 meters ever run by a woman. She qualified for the Olympic team in the 100-meter, 200-meter, and relay.

Wilma began practicing for the Olympics, flying from the starting block in every race. She ran with power and fluid strength. She was usually so far ahead of her competitors that sometimes she would slow down in the middle of a race to avoid completely demolishing her opponents.

But one nagging problem remained—the absence of Yolanda. Wilma hated not seeing her baby, yet she could not go to St. Louis and get back in time to fulfill her class and athletic obligations. When she talked to Yvonne about the problem, Yvonne said something that brought matters quickly to a head. Yvonne said she was growing very attached to Yolanda. Yvonne wanted to adopt the baby and keep her permanently. Wilma panicked. She did not want to lose her daughter.

In spite of her father's orders to stay away from Robert, Wilma went to see him and told him what was happening. Risking her father's anger, Wilma and Robert drove to St. Louis over the holiday break, picked up Yolanda, and brought her home to Clarksville. Fortunately, Wilma's father had recovered his health somewhat. Wilma's parents now agreed to take Yolanda. With the baby living closer, Wilma could come home from Nashville more frequently to see her.

In 1959, Wilma won a silver medal in the 100-meter dash at the Pan-American Games in Chicago, Illinois. She won the AAU title in both the 100-meter and 200-meter races.

Ed Temple was named coach of the United States Olympic track team for the upcoming 1960 Olympics in Rome, Italy. Twenty-year-old Wilma Rudolph now had a chance to get a shiny gold medal. She declared that she intended to become the most famous woman runner in America.[8] She stood to be named the fastest woman runner in the world. She was headed for Rome and a chance at Olympic glory.

5

Rome—1960

The pomp and glory of the 1960 Olympics was under way. The Italian organizing committee, led by President Giulio Onesti, used the awesome stage of historic Rome to lift the Olympic Games to an even greater spectacle.[1] The marathon, a long-distance Olympic race that covered 26 miles and 385 yards (42.2 kilometers), would be run over the Appian Way, a highway built by Appius Claudius Caecus in 312 B.C. It would end at the Arch of Constantine.

The Olympic Village was well prepared to receive the seven thousand athletes coming from eighty-four nations. There were five dining halls, a post office, stores, entertainment centers, and even banks. The Olympic Games would run from August 25 to September 11.

The American Olympic team arrived early. Wilma loved the atmosphere of Rome, especially the warmth of the people. They "always laughed and seemed so jolly," she said.[2] When Wilma got to the Olympic Village, she found that she and other young Americans were very popular. American music and new dance steps were known around the world from the television program *American Bandstand*. The other young athletes were eager to learn all about the music. "They all thought we were the coolest cats," Wilma said.[3] Also on the American team was 1956 silver decathlon winner Rafer Johnson and young boxer Cassius Clay (who later changed his name to Muhammad Ali).

The temperatures in Rome were hovering around one hundred degrees, but that did not bother Wilma. She was used to the hot summers of Tennessee.

Before Wilma could compete in the Olympics, she had to win her trials. Considering the excellent quality of her running, that did not seem to pose much of a problem. But on the Tuesday before the completion, Wilma was just jogging along when she stumbled and fell, hurting her ankle. The team doctor hurried to her side and inspected the damage. He could not assure Wilma that she would be able to compete. He told her to rest the ankle and hope for the best. Fortunately, it turned out to be a strain, and not a sprain or a break, which might have kept her out of the Olympics and could have ended her running career.

While she was resting her ankle, Wilma renewed old friendships she had made during the 1956 Olympics. She also made new friends, including the brash Cassius Clay. When it was time for tryouts on straight, smooth tracks, Wilma Rudolph ran like the champion she was.

On the 100-meter dash, Rudolph's confidence was so high that she took a nap before the second heat. (The trial race before a competition consists of two parts, and each is called a heat.) Wilma had the reputation for loving to sleep and grabbing little catnaps whenever she could.

When it was time for Rudolph's second heat, she burst from the starting block and tied the world record of 11.3 seconds. She had definitely qualified for Olympic competition.

The first black woman to receive an Olympic gold medal was Alice Coachman Davis of the United States in 1948. She won the high jump at the Olympic Games in London, England. In 1956 another black American woman, Mildred McDaniel, brought home the gold for the same event. Wilma Rudolph hoped she would become the third black woman to win an Olympic gold medal.

Alice Coachman Davis does the high jump at the Olympic Games in 1948. Her success paved the way for the next generation of African-American women champions.

Wilma Rudolph's first chance at a gold medal in Rome came in the 100-yard dash. Rudolph said later that an athlete has to be mentally strong to survive the kind of pressure that comes before such a race.[4]

As the thin, graceful young woman waited in the pack for the "get set—go" signal, she was ready. At the start, Wilma sprang from the starting block, but the Russian runner, Maria Itkina, quickly took the lead. At the halfway mark, Rudolph overtook Itkina. Rudolph kept the lead, breaking the finish-line tape three yards ahead of her closest competitor. Rudolph had won the 100-meter dash and her first Olympic gold medal.

"After I won the 100," Rudolph said later, "my thought was . . . home. I wondered if my mom and dad were watching because when I left home we didn't have a television. But they were okay. They were able to see me win and see me get on the stand."[5]

Rudolph's style and speed made her a favorite among the spectators. One Rome reporter described her performance this way: "Running for gold medal glory, Miss Rudolph regularly got away to good starts with her arms pumping in classic style, then smoothly shifted gears to a flowing stride that made the rest of the pack seem to be churning in a treadmill."[6]

The Italians dubbed Rudolph *La Gazzella Nera*, "the Black Gazelle." A gazelle is a graceful antelope known for its speed. The French called her *Perle Noire*, "the Black Pearl." The British press simply called her

Wilma-on-the-wing. "I thought it was wonderful," Rudolph later said. "They were speaking of something beautiful in color and motion."[7]

Rudolph had run the 100-meter dash in just 11.0 seconds. The previous record, set by Australian Shirley Strickland, was 11.3 seconds. Rudolph had set a new world record, but it never appeared in the record books because the wind at her back was too strong. For a world speed record, the wind cannot be stronger than 2.0 meters per second. When Rudolph ran, the wind was 2.75 meters per second.

With one gold medal in hand, Rudolph set out to win another. She was thinking of the awesome performance of her hero, Jesse Owens, in the 1936 Olympics in Berlin, Germany. Adolf Hitler ruled Germany then, and the atmosphere was politically charged. Jesse Owens faced a hostile, taunting German crowd.

Hitler boasted of the powers of the Aryan people—blond, blue-eyed people of northern Europe. He said they were the best athletes in the world because they were members of a super race. Hitler especially hated darker-skinned people. When he learned that German runners would be competing against Jesse Owens, a black American, he was sure that Owens would be soundly beaten. Instead, Owens won the 100-meter dash, the 200-meter dash, and the 400-meter relay. Wilma Rudolph dreamed that, as a special tribute to Owens, she might win those same races in Rome.

Rudolph takes a flying start in the 200-meter sprint.

Rudolph was a favorite in the 200-meter dash. In the first heat, she ran a record Olympic time of 23.2 seconds, easily outdistancing her closest rival, Jutta Heine of Germany. In the final, Rudolph won in 24.0 seconds. The lithe, popular young American now had two gold medals. To equal Jesse Owens's triumph, she had just one more hurdle to leap—the 400-meter relay.

For many people, relay races are among the most exciting events at the Olympics. It is the only team sport in track and field. The four members on each team take turns running, then passing a stick, called a baton, to the next member of the team. The fastest member of the relay team is chosen to be the anchor, running the last lap. In addition to speed, the relay race requires incredible coordination during the baton passing.

There was a lot of attention on Rudolph now. The four Tigerbelles from Tennessee State who would run in the relay were Rudolph, Lucinda Williams, Barbara Jones, and Martha Hudson. During the qualifying heat, in sweltering temperatures, the women set a new world

A winning team: Tennessee Tigerbelles (from left) Wilma Rudolph, Lucinda Williams, Barbara Jones, and Martha Hudson, after earning the gold for the 400-meter relay.

record. In the actual race, they would be competing against strong teams from Germany, Italy, Poland, Great Britain, and the Soviet Union.

Martha Hudson ran the first lap, and Rudolph would run the last. As the baton was being passed to Rudolph for the final leg of the race, the team was ahead by two yards. But Rudolph fumbled the baton handoff. The baton came perilously close to dropping. If it had dropped, the team would have been disqualified. Rudolph recovered quickly, though she had lost precious time during the fumble. As the anchor, Rudolph was responsible for the final lap. Everything depended on her now. The pressure was intense.

Running on the curved relay track would put pressure on Rudolph's injured ankle and might possibly revive the old weakness in her once crippled leg. Rudolph put all this from her mind and concentrated on the run.

The Russian team had moved into the lead as Rudolph began her lap. With a great burst of speed, Rudolph quickly overtook their anchor. For the final ninety meters of the race, Rudolph flew, arms pumping, muscles stretching. She crashed through the finish-line tape, beating Russia's Irina Press by three-tenths of a second. There had not been much distance to spare. The crowd rose to their feet in a deafening roar of approval.

In this moment of amazing triumph, Rudolph

recalled the disappointments she had overcome that led finally to this achievement. After she had time to reflect, she said, "Winning is great, but if you are really going to do something in life, the secret is learning how to lose . . . If you can pick up after a crushing defeat, and go on to win again, you are going to be a champion someday."[8]

Wilma Rudolph stood on the gold medal level of the victory stand as her nation's anthem, "The Star-Spangled Banner," was played. The gold medal was placed around her neck. It was a glorious, stirring moment. But Rudolph was not prepared for what came next.

Immediately after the awards ceremony, mobs surged around her. Microphones were shoved in her face. Everybody wanted to ask her a question, often several people at once. Rudolph heard a babble of excited voices. Finally, American officials of the Olympic Committee hustled her away to a quiet place. Later, at her first major press conference, Rudolph became so upset that she burst into tears. One of the reporters warned her, "Your life will never be the same," and Rudolph said later, "How right he was."[9]

By overcoming her physical disabilities to become the world's fastest woman, Wilma Rudolph had accomplished an inspiring feat of courage. But she was only twenty years old, and she had the rest of her life to live.

Ed Temple described her performance in Rome

Rudolph accepts the Olympic gold medal for the 100-meter dash from Avery Brundage, president of the International Olympic Committee.

this way: "Well, that was the explosion. That's where she exploded and won the three gold medals."[10] Temple was asked whether he had seen Rudolph's spectacular showing coming. He said he knew she was improving, but he did not realize she had become that fast. When asked if Rudolph was performing beyond her potential, he said she had not yet even reached her potential.[11]

Ed Temple made it clear that there was much more to Wilma Rudolph than her athletic skills. He said the most impressive thing about her was "her personality, her charm. These are things that sold Wilma." He said her charisma (special grace which touches people deeply) really captured the imagination of people "not only here in the United States but all over the world."[12]

6

OLYMPIC AFTERGLOW

After the great triumph at the Rome Olympics, Wilma Rudolph was invited to the Vatican, in Vatican City, Italy. There, she and her American teammates viewed the architectural and artistic wonders of the pope's headquarters. Then they were ushered into Pope John XXIII's presence. As a Southern Baptist, Rudolph did not know what to expect from the head of the Roman Catholic Church. Everybody in the party was speaking in whispers, so Rudolph had the sense that this was a very important occasion.

The minute the elderly pope appeared, the mood

changed. "Pope John was a real jolly fellow," Rudolph said later. "He had rosy cheeks and he laughed a lot. He was a very happy and vibrant man. Everybody around him looked happy."[1] The pope spoke to each of the athletes, and he told them they were all wonderful no matter if they won or lost.

After the impressive closing ceremonies of the Olympics, Rudolph and the other Tigerbelles traveled to Great Britain to take part in the British Empire Games in London. Rudolph was victorious in all the races she entered.

The attention of the press was relentless. It focused entirely on Rudolph, and the other Tigerbelles were ignored. Rudolph noticed the tension in the group. Coach Temple tried to smooth things over, but it was unavoidable that the other three girls would feel hurt. Their athletic achievements were not being celebrated. All the fame was going to Rudolph. Rudolph was learning another hard lesson. The price of fame sometimes cost a person friendships.

From London, Rudolph and the team traveled to Stuttgart, West Germany, and to Cologne on the German border with France. Everywhere Rudolph appeared, she was mobbed. Mounted police struggled to keep the fans contained in Cologne. In Berlin, excited admirers surrounded the bus on which Rudolph was riding. They pounded on the bus with their fists until they got their wave from Wilma

Rudolph, and then they allowed the bus to continue on its way. Coach Temple, seeing the way people were responding to Rudolph, noted, "She's done more for her country than what the U.S. could have paid her for."[2]

When it was finally time to return to the United States, Wilma Rudolph had no idea what was waiting for her. She had planned to go directly home to Clarksville for a long-awaited reunion with her family. But when she stepped off the plane in Nashville, Tennessee, she was told she had to stay for a while in Nashville so the people in her hometown could complete their plans for welcoming her home.

Even in Nashville, a huge crowd greeted Rudolph at the airport. Rudolph saw mayors, governors, the Tennessee State University marching band, and many journalists. But she was so homesick, she only wanted to see the faces of her loved ones, and she did not want to wait. In her college dorm that night, Wilma pleaded with some friends to drive her to Clarksville. In the middle of the night, Rudolph and her parents had a happy private reunion amidst hugs and tears. Then Rudolph's friends returned her to the dorm at Tennessee State, and nobody was the wiser.

Clarksville was very excited about its famous daughter. The town was planning a big parade. In all town parades, the marchers and the spectators were segregated according to race. Blacks and whites did not mingle, even at outdoor events. Rudolph was thrilled that her hometown wanted to give her a parade, but she did not want a segregated parade. She had painful memories of segregation as she and her mother rode those buses to Nashville for her physical therapy. They always had to sit in the back of the bus, while the white people sat in the front. In fact, experiencing the realities of segregation when she was a child, Rudolph sometimes thought that "all white people were mean and evil."[3]

Rudolph's religious faith was so strong that she never grew bitter. But she did not want to be honored in her hometown by a segregated parade. She insisted that the parade be integrated. So when Clarksville's welcome home parade for Wilma Rudolph got under way, it was the first integrated parade in the city's history.[4] The parade began about two miles outside the city, with motorcycle police leading the car containing Wilma Rudolph toward town. Another car joined the parade at the head of the column. In this car rode Rudolph's parents, an older brother and his family, and baby Yolanda. As they neared downtown Clarksville, Rudolph was amazed at the throngs of people lining the route. It looked as if every single resident of Clarksville had turned out to welcome her home.

Marching together were the all-white American Legion, Elks, and the Veterans of Foreign Wars, along with all the traditional black groups, pastors of the area churches, black fraternal organizations, and black marching bands. Rudolph looked out at the amazing sight. It was as if segregation had taken a holiday for this occasion.

After the parade, Rudolph went to the Clarksville Armory for a banquet in her honor. An elderly white judge, William Hudson, stood up to comment on the integrated banquet. "The absolute best music comes out of that piano when you play both the black keys and the white keys together," he said, to the applause of everyone present.[5]

It was a stirring tribute to the love that everyone felt for Wilma Rudolph. Many black people there remembered her as a disabled little girl, and now they rejoiced in her triumph. The people at the banquet were able to put aside their prejudices and share in the pride in a local girl who had captured the hearts of the world. Wilma Rudolph had brought Clarksville together.

After a short rest with her family, Rudolph was invited to Chicago to receive the keys to the city from Mayor Richard Daley. She was celebrated in public rallies in Detroit, Michigan; Atlanta, Georgia; and Philadelphia, Pennsylvania. She attended many parties with the rich and famous. She found herself making small talk with famous celebrities like Harry Belafonte, the actor and singer, and Lena Horne, the film star.

Next, Rudolph was invited to Washington, D.C., where she met first with Vice President Lyndon Johnson. Johnson presented her with a bottle of perfume. Then she was ushered into the Oval Office for a meeting with President John F. Kennedy.

Rudolph and her mother waited in the Oval Office for President Kennedy to arrive. What happened next shocked everyone there. President Kennedy entered the room and invited his guests to sit down, and he began to do the same. But somebody had moved

The new Olympic star meets John F. Kennedy, president of the United States.

President Kennedy's favorite rocker from its usual spot. As he backed up to sit down, he fell to the floor. Everyone knew that President Kennedy suffered from major back problems, and the accident aroused fears that he may have seriously injured himself. But the Secret Service men helped the president to his feet, and he began laughing so heartily that everyone was put at ease. President Kennedy spent the next thirty-five minutes talking to Wilma Rudolph and her mother. President Kennedy said, "It's really an honor to meet you and tell you what a magnificent runner you are."[6] It was a memorable moment in Rudolph's life.

After the meeting with President Kennedy, the whirlwind of banquets, television appearances, and speeches continued. Rudolph was honored at a New York City banquet hosted by the National Association for the Advancement of Colored People (NAACP). NAACP president Roy Wilkins praised her in a speech. Rudolph showed poise and patience at all these events, and she gave autographs to hundreds of fans wherever she went.

Unfortunately, Rudolph's Olympic success did not help her family's financial troubles. Today, many Olympic winners receive large sums of money to become spokespeople for large companies. Often the fame and money earned from these product endorsements make the athletes celebrated and wealthy.

Today, a beautiful young woman like Wilma Rudolph would be in demand to advertise any number of products, from athletic equipment to automobiles. In 1960, this was not the case.

Wilma Rudolph was an amateur, and that meant she could not profit from her Olympic triumph. As Coach Temple put it, "Wilma couldn't even get a pencil, couldn't even get a pair of shoes."[7] He related how, when Rudolph was winning the gold medals in Rome, her parents had no television set. Somebody found out about this, and one was donated to them. But the Rudolphs had to refuse the gift. Wilma Rudolph was not permitted to receive any gifts or compensation from her career—and neither could her family. If Rudolph or her family had accepted anything, she could never have competed again as an amateur.

In the autumn of 1960, as the nation continued to shower praise on her, Wilma Rudolph went to Louisville, Kentucky, to join a friend—another young Olympian—in his victory celebrations. Unlike Rudolph, who was shy and quiet, this Olympian was making the most of his celebrity. At the Olympic Village in Rome, eighteen-year-old Cassius Clay and twenty-year-old Rudolph had become friends. Clay won the gold medal for the light heavyweight division by defeating a Polish boxer.

"I can still see him strutting around the village with his gold medal on," Rudolph later said. "He slept with it. He went to the cafeteria with it. He never took it off."[8] Rudolph liked Clay, and she followed him around, waiting to see what he would do next. It was always exciting where he was. Now Clay invited Rudolph to climb into his pink Cadillac and ride with him down Walnut Street in the west end of Louisville. Like Clarksville, Louisville was segregated, and they were driving in the black neighborhood.

Clay stopped at every intersection to shout to the people on the sidewalk, "I'm Cassius Clay! I am the greatest!"[9] Sitting beside him, Rudolph sank deeper into the passenger seat, nearing the floor.

Clay stood up in the convertible and, after he announced himself, he would shout, "And this is Wilma Rudolph. She is the greatest!" Rudolph pleaded with Clay to sit down, but he demanded, "Wilma, stand up!"[10] Rudolph covered her face with her hands. Undaunted, Clay shouted even louder, "Here she is down here. It's Wilma Rudolph. She is the greatest!"[11] Finally, Rudolph gave up and stood up beside Clay in the pink convertible to the screams and cheers of the gathering crowd. They were both very attractive young people in their primes, looking just like what they were—champions. Later, Rudolph said of Clay, "I saw him at the very beginning. It was bedlam. I always told him, 'You should be on stage.'"[12]

Wilma Rudolph, the quiet Clarksville girl, had been swept into an unreal world she had never imagined in

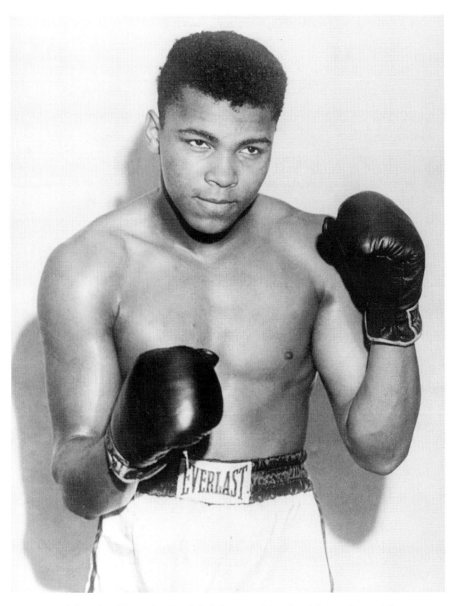

After the Olympics, Rudolph became friends with another gold medal winner: Cassius Clay—the boxer who later became world-famous as Muhammad Ali.

her wildest fantasies. She was having experiences that seemed more like a fairytale than real life. It was hard to take it all in. She received ticker-tape parades—millions of pieces of confetti would rain down on her from the windows of tall buildings. She was treated like a star, but she received no money for any of it. She later said, "You become world famous and you sit with kings and queens," but then, suddenly, it is all over and you are back in the real world. "You can't go back to living the way you did before because you've been taken out of one setting and shown the other. That becomes a struggle and makes *you* struggle."[13]

Wilma Rudolph was chosen Female Athlete of the Year for 1960 by the Associated Press. It was a grand finale to the most dramatic year in her young life. She also won the 1960 Helms Athletic Foundation World Trophy for the North American continent and was named the winner of the *Los Angeles Times* award for success in women's track and field.

The classroom at Tennessee State waited for her to come back and finish her education. It was still a financial struggle to keep going to school and support Yolanda. Like Cinderella whose carriage was turning into a pumpkin, Wilma Rudolph, the Olympic gold medalist, was returning to reality.

7

RETIREMENT AND MARRIAGE

 n February 1961, the New York Athletic Club track meet took place at Madison Square Garden in New York City. Wilma Rudolph broke her record for the 60-yard dash. She ran the race in 6.8 seconds. She then claimed the world record of 7.8 seconds in the 70-yard dash. Wilma Rudolph had not taken time off to rest on her Olympic laurels. In Columbus, Ohio, in March 1961, she won the 100-yard dash in 10.8 seconds at the Women's AAU Indoor Championships. It was a United States record. She then set a world record during the trial heat for the 220-yard dash, taking only 25.0 seconds to go the distance.

Rudolph sprints across the finish line at Madison Square Garden in 1961.

At another meet in Louisville, Kentucky, Rudolph broke the speed record that had stood for twenty-six years in the 70-yard dash. The record was 8.2 seconds, and Rudolph shaved off 0.6 second. In July, she ran the 100-yard dash in the United States Women's Outdoor Championship meet in Gary, Indiana, in just 10.8 seconds. Then she set a new world record of 11.2 seconds in the 100-meter dash in West Germany. Next, Wilma Rudolph was off to Stanford University in Palo Alto, California, for a competition with

Russian women. At the time, Rudolph was beginning to think about retirement. She wanted to finish her competitive career with a big win.

Rudolph was scheduled to run the 100-meter dash and anchor the U.S. relay team in the 400 meters. She had no problem winning the 100-meter dash in 11.3 seconds, but the relay race proved to be a challenge. By the time Rudolph got the baton from her teammate, the Russian women were far ahead. Rudolph put everything she had in the last lap. She was gaining on the Russians. She later recalled that she saw the Russian runner looking back, surprised at how quickly Rudolph was closing the gap between them. Rudolph caught and passed her opponent and went on to win the race for the United States. The crowd cheered her amazing come-from-behind win.

Fans surged around Rudolph, asking for her autograph. One small boy especially touched her heart. When he asked for her autograph, Rudolph impulsively removed her track shoes and signed both of them. Then she handed them to the boy. He said, "Really? Really? You're giving me your track shoes?" When Rudolph said yes, he ran away clutching the shoes and calling back to her, "Thank you, thank you, thank you."[1]

During the months since Wilma Rudolph had returned from the Olympics, her father's health had been failing. Edward Rudolph was diabetic, and on the night of Wilma's welcome-home banquet, he had collapsed. Not wanting to spoil his daughter's big night, he assured everyone he was all right. He refused to be taken home, insisting, "I'm all right, just leave me alone."[2] During the final months of 1960 and into the spring of 1961, Edward Rudolph grew slowly weaker. He told Wilma to go on with her life and not to worry about him. She tried to do that. In April 1961, Wilma's father died. It was a painful blow to Wilma.

Wilma Rudolph was awarded the Amateur Athletic Union's 1961 Sullivan Award, which is given annually to the outstanding amateur athlete of that year. The inscription on the Sullivan trophy read, "To the athlete, male or female, who by performance, example, and good influence did the most to advance the cause of good sportsmanship." The James E. Sullivan Memorial Trophy is named for the former president of the AAU. It was established in 1930. In the thirty-one-year history of the Sullivan trophy up to 1961, only two other women had won the honor—Ann Curtis for swimming in 1941, and Patricia McCormick for diving in 1956.

In 1962, Rudolph received the Babe Didrikson Zaharias Award as the most outstanding female athlete of the world. Commenting on her great success and the honors bestowed on her, Olympian Jesse Owens said some years later, "Wilma Rudolph's courage and her triumph over her physical handicaps are among

Babe Didrickson Zaharius (1911?–1956) is often called the greatest woman athlete in history. She set world records in track and field events at the 1932 Olympics, then went on to become a famous golfer.

the most inspiring jewels in the crown of Olympic sports. . . . She was speed and motion incarnate, the most beautiful image ever seen on the track."[3]

After winning just about every race she could enter, Wilma Rudolph retired from competition in 1962. She wanted to quit at the peak of her career. She decided not to compete in the 1964 Olympics, saying, "The best I could do if I went back is win three gold medals again. If I won two, there would be something lacking. I'll stick with the glory won—like Jesse Owens did in 1936."[4]

Rudolph graduated from Tennessee A & I on May 27, 1963, with a degree in elementary education. She made several more goodwill trips overseas. She gave talks to young people describing how she worked hard on her goals and achieved success. She urged them to do the same.

Rudolph traveled to French West Africa for the U.S. State Department and gave inspirational talks to young people. It was a great thrill for her to see Africa for the first time, and to learn about the native culture of her ancestors. Rudolph also traveled to Japan with the Reverend Billy Graham Baptist Christian Athletes Group.

After the trip, Rudolph returned to Clarksville and followed her usual custom of visiting her former high school coach, Clinton Gray. Gray had become a dear friend. It was then that she learned the sad news that

Coach Gray had been killed in a car accident. Rudolph wrote a special letter to be read at Coach Gray's funeral. The loss reminded her of her sadness when her friend Nancy Bowen died in the auto accident on prom night.

In a bittersweet turn of events, Wilma Rudolph was offered Coach Gray's job as girls' track coach at Burt High School. She was also offered a job as a second-grade teacher at Cobb Elementary School, where she had gone as a child. With the income from both positions, Rudolph could earn a modest living.

Now that her career plans were set, Rudolph's attention turned to her personal life. She had known Robert Eldridge since she was a little girl. She had always liked him, and he was the father of their little girl. During the busy years of training for the Olympics and other competitions, Rudolph and Eldridge had drifted apart. Wilma's father had not approved of Eldridge, so that, too, had been a barrier to their relationship. But now there was no reason for them to be apart, and they made plans to get married.

On July 20, 1963, Wilma Rudolph and Robert Eldridge were married in an unusual ceremony. The young couple could not find a church in Clarksville large enough for all their guests. They ended up having an outdoor wedding. It was arranged by a friend of Wilma's who was a florist. A big open field near the Rudolph home was chosen, and the florist made it look like the inside of a church. There was an altar, flowers, and rows of chairs. All the flowers were pale blue. A huge crowd of family and friends came to see the couple become man and wife. Afterward, there was a small family reception at Rudolph's mother's home, and a bigger reception in the American Legion hall.

The newly married couple could not afford a honeymoon. Instead they went to a family reunion of the Eldridge clan as their wedding trip. Rudolph had the chance to meet many of her husband's relatives whom she had never met before.

Robert Eldridge enrolled in Tennessee State, and twenty-three-year-old Wilma Rudolph prepared to begin her career as a teacher and a coach. The couple was starting married life with very little money, a problem that would continue.

Wilma Rudolph had been honored and celebrated all over the world, and most people knew her name and the inspiring story of her Olympic triumph. She had been treated like royalty at banquets and parades. But she never enjoyed a luxurious lifestyle. "I was besieged with money problems," Rudolph said later. "People were always expecting me to be a star, but I wasn't making the money to live like one."[5]

8

Career and Motherhood

 n September 1963, Wilma Rudolph began teaching at Cobb Elementary School. It was a strange experience for the young woman to return to her childhood school and find the same principal who had been there when she was a student. In fact, Rudolph would be working with one of the teachers who had taught her. Rudolph was also coaching at Burt High School, working with young girls, just as her mentor, Coach Gray, had worked with the girls of her generation.

Rudolph loved the children and enjoyed teaching, but there were problems from the start. She had studied elementary education at Tennessee State. She was very enthusiastic about the new techniques she had learned and was anxious to put them into practice. But the teachers at Cobb Elementary School liked the traditional methods they had been using for years.

Wilma Rudolph was in a difficult position. The newcomer wanted to make some changes in the time-honored system. Everybody remembered little Wilma Rudolph. Now, here she was, trying to tell them how to teach. They had been teaching for decades, and she was a brand-new teacher. The establishment at Cobb Elementary was a bit annoyed, and Rudolph was frustrated.

Adding to the stress in Rudolph's life was the fact that she was the sole supporter of the family. Her husband was going to college, and they had a child. The bills piled up, and Rudolph's modest income, even from two jobs, did not go far. Her $400 a month was not enough.

During the school year, Rudolph became pregnant with her second child. Daughter Djuana was born on May 19, 1964. Now Rudolph had two children to support.

When the 1964 school year began in September, Rudolph was back at Cobb Elementary and Burt High School. She tried to adjust to her fellow teachers, and she delighted in the children.

In August 1965, a son, Robert Jr., was born. When

he first saw the baby, her husband said, "Hey, I finally got a dude."[1] From then on, the boy's nickname was Dude.

With three children to care for, it was impossible for Rudolph to continue teaching and coaching. The family needed more money, and Rudolph was hoping to find a higher-paying position. Her husband was still in college, so the burden of supporting the family continued to fall solely on Wilma.

Rudolph was offered a job in Evansville, Indiana, as director of a community center. The family packed up and moved to Indiana. But the job was a disappointment. Rudolph did not believe she could be happy there. The family had to move again—this time to Poland Springs, Maine. Rudolph was hired by the Job Corps at a government center. The Job Corps was part of President Lyndon Johnson's outreach to disadvantaged young people. They received training in job skills in centers removed from the drug- and crime-infested neighborhoods they lived in.

Wilma Rudolph's job was to run the girls' physical education program. She wrote curricula for the program and decided what sports would be emphasized. She ran the exercise classes for the girls. Rudolph enjoyed interacting with the young women and offering them her unique perspective as a girl from a poor background who rose to dramatic success. But still, it was not exactly what Rudolph wanted. Like many government programs, the Job Corps had too much regulation. Rudolph had hoped for more freedom in planning programs and working with youth. She worked there for a year, but then another opportunity came along.

In 1967, President Johnson started a major effort to help poor young people. It was called Operation Champ. The United States government was investing $1 million for a ten-city program focusing on great athletes working as motivators for youth. Each city received $100,000 to set up the program. More than 250,000 young people participated in the program. As part of Operation Champ, the Department of Labor provided each city with 250 Youth Corps workers, as well as senior counselors.

The cities targeted were New York, Detroit, Washington, D.C., Los Angeles, Houston, San Antonio, Pittsburgh, St. Louis, Baltimore, and Boston. Wilma Rudolph was asked to be one of the sports champions taking part in the program. She would have to travel to all the cities and give motivational talks to youth.[2]

Some of the other athletes who joined Rudolph in this effort were Olympic gold medal swimmer Donna de Varona, heavyweight boxing champion Rocky Marciano, and Ralph Boston, another Tennessee State track star.

Wilma Rudolph really appreciated the chance to share her enthusiasm with young people. She was an excellent speaker, exciting and warm. "I don't consciously try to be a role model," she said later, "so I don't know if I am or not. That's for others to decide."[3] Rudolph traveled to all the cities, and she taught track-and-field skills along with the important life lessons she had learned from her parents, teachers, coaches, and experiences.

While she worked in Operation Champ, Rudolph's family lived in Poland Springs, Maine. Rudolph wanted to be closer to her relatives in Tennessee, so she asked for a transfer. She was then based in St. Louis, and her family lived there as she traveled around the country. Very soon after that, Rudolph's younger sister, Charlene, who lived in Detroit, was taken ill. Rudolph wanted to help care for her, so the family moved again—to Detroit. Rudolph got a teaching job at Pelham Junior High School, in the middle of the black neighborhood.

"The kids there were terrific," Wilma Rudolph later said of her students at Pelham. "All they needed were outlets, and I gave them one through track."[4] Rudolph remained at Pelham Junior High School for a year and a half. She felt she had done a lot of good, but she continued to feel she had not found the right niche. Charlene Rudolph was now feeling better, and Wilma was ready for another change.

It was now 1968, a time of great turmoil in the United States. There was much unrest over American involvement in the Vietnam War. There was racial strife all over America as Dr. Martin Luther King, Jr., and other civil rights activists worked to correct injustices and gain equality for black Americans. On the night that Wilma Rudolph and her children were traveling from Detroit to Nashville to attend an aunt's funeral, Dr. King was assassinated in Memphis, Tennessee. Rudolph heard of the death of King on the plane as it came into Nashville. Rudolph later said there was great shock and tension on the plane.[5]

Rudolph and her children landed in Nashville and went to the bus station for the trip to Clarksville. As they sat in the bus terminal, a white man suddenly walked up and spat on Rudolph's children. Nearby, a black man witnessed the incident and called the police, who came and arrested the attacker. Rudolph was already grieving her aunt and Dr. King when the ugly incident took place. It plunged her into depression. Later, she called that day "the absolute low point of my life."[6]

It had been eight years since the glory days of the Olympics. Twenty-eight-year-old Wilma Rudolph had worked at several jobs. She had found some fulfillment, but all the jobs ended up disappointing her. She had the feeling that she was hired for most of them only because of her name and that her employers did not expect her to be more than a figurehead.

Using the modest savings she had, Wilma Rudolph

Rudolph greatly admired Dr. Martin Luther King, Jr., and she was devastated by his assassination.

spent some time at home with her children. Yolanda was now thirteen, and her mother was coaching her in running. However, Yolanda did not appear to have the natural ability to go far in the sport. Djuana was tall and thin like her mother, but she was not at all interested in running. Robert Jr. loved football more than anything else.

In 1971, son Xurry was born. Rudolph's husband was not working, and the pressure was on for her to get employment. A good friend, Boston Celtics basketball player Bill Russell, advised Rudolph to try something totally new.[7] So when Xurry was old enough to be cared for by his father, Wilma Rudolph headed for Los Angeles, California, alone.

Rudolph was immediately hired by the Watts Community Action Committee. She then sent for her family to join her in Los Angeles. Unfortunately, her salary was very low, and a worried Rudolph asked

This family picture was taken in 1976. From right are Wilma and her husband, Robert, with Djuana, 12; Robert, 10; Xurry, 5; and Yolanda, 17. Standing behind Yolanda is Anthony Eldridge, 19.

herself, "How can you support a family on peanuts?"[8] She looked for another job and was hired by the University of California at Los Angeles as an administrator for the Department of Afro-American Studies. The job did not last long, and once more Wilma Rudolph was out of work. She received an invitation from Mayor Richard Daley to work in Chicago, Illinois. She would work at Daley's Youth Foundation. As it turned out, the salary was not what she had been promised, so she quit. "I felt exploited," Rudolph later said, talking about the many jobs she had taken with high hopes, only to be given little money and few real responsibilities.[9]

Wilma Rudolph learned of a fund-raising effort in Charleston, West Virginia, to raise a million dollars for a track-and-field hall of fame. She believed in the project and spent some time helping reach the goal. When the drive was successful, she returned home. She was deeply in debt, and her husband was very ill.

Rudolph received a contract to write an autobiography, and with the proceeds the family was able to move to a nice home in the suburbs of Clarksville. The book, *Wilma: The Story of Wilma Rudolph*, was successful and was made into a television movie starring Shirley Jo Finney as the adult Rudolph. It was a powerful drama about how Wilma Rudolph ran against the odds and won.

Daughter Yolanda began enjoying running even

though she was a barely average racer. She attended Tennessee State and, like her mother, was coached by Ed Temple. Robert Jr. and Djuana were in high school and Xurry was in elementary school as the 1970s came to a close.

For a long time, Wilma Rudolph had sought meaningful work where she could really use her talents. She had finally come to the conclusion that it was not going to happen unless she made it happen herself. She needed to take her future into her own hands. From that determination sprang the idea of the Wilma Rudolph Foundation.

9

THE FOUNDATION AND THE LAST WALK

he Wilma Rudolph Foundation was established in 1982 to train young athletes for national and international competition. But Wilma Rudolph wanted to do much more. She wanted to spare them some of the difficulties she had had to struggle with. She had learned the hard way how great a challenge it is to cope with sudden fame. She had gone from being an ordinary young woman to a whirlwind celebrity, and then back again to the real world. Once the trophies were sitting on the shelves and the applause had stopped, an athlete had to live the rest of her life. Rudolph wanted these young athletes to be better prepared than she had been. Being a "superstar" for a little while was not enough to build a life on, she would tell the young people.[1]

Rudolph had always been eager to work with young people and give them the benefit of her own experience. With her foundation, she could finally do it in her own way. "I would be very disappointed," she said, "if I were only to be remembered as a runner."[2] She wanted her legacy to be the work she had done for youth.

Referring to the foundation, former Tigerbelle teammate Isabelle Daniels Holston said everyone around Wilma Rudolph always knew she would do more with her life than just rest on her Olympic laurels. "She was born to inspire, to love, and to give," Holston said. "She did, not only to the people of America but to the world."[3]

The Wilma Rudolph Foundation had a file on every young athlete it registered, keeping track not only of their athletic progress, but also of their academic success. Rudolph never wanted education to be shortchanged in the pursuit of athletic glory. In many motivational talks to young people, Rudolph told them how important it was for them to be themselves and to believe in themselves. Her most powerful message was to remind them that the road to any success was not easy. "The triumph can't be had without the struggle," she told them.[4]

In her many speeches to college students, Rudolph talked about women in sports.

Based in Indianapolis, Indiana, the Wilma Rudolph Foundation had more than a thousand participants in 1985. Free coaching was offered to young athletes in whatever sports they chose. They were prepared for AAU meets and for the Olympics if they wanted to compete internationally. The foundation used the facilities of high schools and colleges for their training. Rudolph told her own story to the athletes to illustrate her lessons. She would often describe herself as "a hardworking lady with certain beliefs."[5]

Wilma Rudolph traveled all over the United States on behalf of her foundation. She enjoyed giving talks to youth and interacting with them. "It's the motherly instinct in me," she said.[6]

Rudolph was also a motivational speaker for adult groups. She had a warm, magnetic personality that touched the hearts of her listeners. Rudolph herself had experienced many of the problems and heartaches of women of her generation, and she was sought out as a speaker for women's groups. The financial and emotional pressures of life had led to the divorce of Rudolph and her husband, Robert Eldridge. Like so many American women, she had become a single mother, coping alone.

In April 1986, Wilma Rudolph was invited to be the keynote speaker at a women's conference organized by California state senator William Campbell. Four thousand women attended the event. Many of them were planning mid-life career changes or confronting broken marriages, and they were looking for courage and inspiration. So many signed up to hear Wilma Rudolph that a second session had to be added to accommodate them all. Rudolph's theme was "Anything that anybody in this room wants to accomplish, you can. But you have to believe it."[7]

Rudolph told the women of her own struggles against disability, poverty, prejudice, and the stress of being the working mother of four children. She said that the same determination that made her a great athlete could make any woman "the best lawyer, doctor or secretary."[8] At the end of her speech, Rudolph received a standing ovation. She spent an hour signing autographs. Deeply moved by this warm reception, she said she was touched to see that her life's accomplishments were appreciated by so many people, and that it meant something to them to spend time with her.[9]

In 1991, Wilma Rudolph was chosen to represent the United States at the celebration of freedom that followed the removal of the Berlin Wall in Germany. In August 1961, East Germans had built a wall across the city of Berlin to separate East Germany from West Germany. Armed guards prevented the East Germans from crossing over to West Berlin, where there was freedom and more opportunity. The wall had stood until 1989, and when it finally came down, the people of both sides of Germany were reunited. Wilma Rudolph, the great Olympian who represented the ideals of world brotherhood, was the perfect choice to be there on behalf of the United States.

Wilma Rudolph had served as a consultant on minority affairs at DePauw University in Greencastle, Indiana, during the 1980s. She remained very active in the sorority she had joined as a sophomore at Tennessee State—Delta Sigma Theta—and she was a willing participant in many worthy causes. As her children were now young adults, married with children of their own, Wilma Rudolph had become a proud grandmother. By the mid-1990s, Rudolph had seven grandchildren.

Later in 1991, Wilma Rudolph learned of yet another project for which she was uniquely qualified to assist. An energetic African-American woman, Byllye Avery, had been working to improve the health of black people. She was dealing with problems that were more severe in blacks than in whites, such as obesity-related diabetes. The calorie-rich and nutritionally weak diets of poor people often added another burden to their already difficult lives. Unhealthy food is cheaper and often more convenient, and Avery wanted to get the message across that lack of exercise and poor diets were killing people. She had launched the Black Women's Health Project in 1980, conducting programs in disease prevention and detection all over America and the world. In 1991, she started a program called Walking for Wellness. She hoped to encourage black women and children to walk for health and fitness. Avery needed a sparkling personality to capture the imagination of the people, someone who was a living symbol of physical fitness. She found that person in Wilma Rudolph, who was eager to help.

Wilma Rudolph was always an advocate for fitness, and she admired Avery's work. In the summer of 1992, Walking for Wellness was launched in Eatonville, Florida. Everyone wore buttons proudly proclaiming that they would "walk with Wilma." Rudolph was at the head of the march. They walked all through the small town, thrilled to be with the Olympic athlete. Avery later recalled one incident that illustrated the spirit and personality of Wilma Rudolph.

"I'll never forget Wilma taking the hand of this little child who had to go to the bathroom, leading him into somebody's house. That's just the kind of person she was."[10] Wilma Rudolph continued to be an enthusiastic participant in the program the rest of her life.

Reflecting her commitment to health, Rudolph was also active in the health and fitness program at Baptist Hospital in Nashville, Tennessee.

In June 1993, Wilma Rudolph was one of the first Americans to be given the newly minted National Sports Award by President Bill Clinton. These athletes, called "the great ones," included golfer Arnold Palmer, basketball player Kareem Abdul-Jabbar, boxer Muhammad Ali, baseball player Ted Williams, and Wilma Rudolph. Rudolph and the others were honored at a White House dinner and at a tribute at Constitution Hall in Washington, D.C.

In May 1994, Blanche Rudolph, Wilma's mother, died. She had been a strong force in her daughter's life from the earliest days, when her encouragement and steadfast faith bolstered Wilma's struggle against her disability. It was a deep loss to Rudolph, but she continued with her active life trying to help others.

Rudolph was invited to the White House by President Bill Clinton on June 20, 1993.

Throughout Wilma Rudolph's life, she always looked forward with hope.

Rudolph continued her work with the Wilma Rudolph Foundation, and she participated in Walking for Wellness events. She took part in walks in Detroit and promised to be in Atlanta on the tenth anniversary of the establishment of the National Black Women's Health Project for a breakfast, in June 1994.

On the morning of the event, Rudolph had a severe headache. She could not take part in the walk, but she struggled to fulfill her commitment as speaker at the breakfast. As she began her remarks, everyone in the room could see she was in distress. The gravity of her physical condition became obvious when she kept repeating the same phrases. Rudolph cut the speech short. This would prove to be her last public appearance.

Wilma Rudolph went to a doctor, who diagnosed her with brain cancer. She was told she did not have much time left.

Rudolph joins four fellow athletes as they receive the National Sports Award from President Clinton. From left, Kareem Abdul-Jabar, Muhammad Ali, Arnold Palmer, Wilma Rudolph, Jeanne Ashe (widow of tennis great Arthur Ashe), and First Lady Hillary Clinton.

Over the next few months, Rudolph was in and out of hospitals. During one period when she was able to go home for several weeks, Rudolph often visited her old coach, Ed Temple. Arm in arm they walked on the Tigerbelle track on which she had run decades earlier. They always chose the early morning hours when they could be alone with their shared memories.

Wilma Rudolph lived for five months after the diagnosis. When she was released from the hospital for the last time, she was gravely ill, and the sad news of her condition spread. The United States Olympic Congress, led by President LeRoy Walker, honored her with a moment of silence. On November 12, 1994, surrounded by family and friends, Wilma Rudolph died in Brentwood, Tennessee. She was fifty-four years old.

William C. Rhoden, writing in the Fort Lauderdale *Sun-Sentinel*, called Rudolph an "American heroine," describing her as "tall, graceful, flowing," a woman who exemplified "the concept of femininity in athletics."[11] In *The Kansas City Star*, Claude Lewis called Rudolph "an athletic queen who mesmerized the international sporting world through personal achievement, physical heroics, and stunning elegance that dwarfed her impoverished beginnings."[12]

On November 17, four thousand people gathered in Tennessee State University's Kean Hall to honor Wilma Rudolph in a memorial service, and many more lined the two-mile-long procession route. Ed Temple commented on the huge crowd. "We got people coming from Rome, from Germany," he said, and from "all over the United States."[13] Eight hundred pupils at St. Bethlehem Elementary School stood at the chain-link fence to watch the funeral procession go by. Ordinary people waved small American flags and bowed their heads. Rudolph's grandchildren wrote a special tribute to her titled "Meme," their pet name for their grandmother. The tribute closed with these words: "She is probably getting fitted for her wings. And, I bet she will be the fastest angel up there. She will be the first woman to receive three gold wings."[14]

After the service at Clarksville's First Baptist Church, Wilma Rudolph was carried by eleven classmates from the Burt High School class of 1958. She was interred at Foston Memorial Gardens in Clarksville, Tennessee. Later a black marble marker was placed over her grave.

10

THE LEGACY OF
A CHAMPION

ollowing her death, tributes to Wilma Rudolph came from all over the world. "She's a legend in track and field, like Jesse Owens," said Ollan Cassell, executive director of USA Track and Field, the official organization for the sport. "After Jesse died, she became the icon, a symbol of what the Olympics mean to this country and this sport."[1] He added that Rudolph cleared a path for other young women in track and field who must always be indebted to her as a pioneer.

Fellow track stars came forward to describe the impact Rudolph had on their lives. Florence

Griffith-Joyner, Olympic gold medalist, said that Rudolph not only inspired her to become a great runner, but taught her "how to go the distance in life."[2] Valerie Brisco-Hooks, 1984 gold medalist, said her career began when her coach at Locke High School in Los Angeles gave her a copy of Rudolph's book, *Wilma*. The fifteen-year-old Valerie Brisco was so inspired that she began to run seriously.[3] Anita De Frantz, a bronze-medal Olympian and member of the U.S. Olympic Committee, called Rudolph "my 'she-ro'."[4]

In 1994, a section of Highway 79 in Clarksville, Tennessee, was renamed Wilma Rudolph Boulevard. In August 1995, Rudolph's alma mater, Tennessee State University, dedicated the newly built six-story dormitory as the Wilma Rudolph Residence Center. In 1996, a life-sized bronze statue of Rudolph was completed and now stands at the Customs House Museum and Cultural Center in Clarksville.

On June 20, 1997, Tennessee governor Don Sundquist proclaimed June 23, her birthday, as Wilma Rudolph Day in Tennessee. Sundquist praised Rudolph for never allowing her disabilities to deter her dreams. He said she will always be remembered for her determination and "always standing with her head held high."[5] In the same month, Byllye Avery held another Walk for Wellness in Baltimore, Maryland. When thousands of people came out in the driving rain, Avery attributed it to Rudolph's spirit. "I know Wilma was there," she said.[6]

On October 23, 1997, Congresswoman Carolyn Kilpatrick of Michigan introduced legislation giving a Congressional Gold Medal honoring the work and achievement of Wilma Rudolph. "The effort and example of Wilma Rudolph helped to blaze the trail that resulted in Title IX today," Kilpatrick said.[7] Title IX is the law that provides equal funding for women's athletics, which were traditionally underfunded so that men's athletics could get more support. Fittingly, Title IX was enacted on June 23, 1972, on Rudolph's birthday. Though Rudolph did not campaign for the law, her athletic triumphs showed the world how important women's athletics are. Kilpatrick said of Rudolph, "Her life truly embodies the American values of hard work, determination, and love of humanity."[8]

There have been many awards established around the country, both large and small, to honor the memory of Wilma Rudolph. On March 30, 2001, the Police Athletic League of Nashville, Tennessee, established the Wilma Rudolph Track Club for boys and girls from nine to fourteen. Youngsters from seventeen Nashville elementary and middle schools were involved. Charlene Rudolph, Wilma's younger sister, and Ed Temple, her beloved mentor and coach, spoke on opening day about how much the club reflected what Rudolph always tried to do. The club provides

Wilma Rudolph overcame tremendous odds to achieve success as an athlete and as an inspirational leader.

tutoring to help students academically, along with exciting athletic competitions.[9]

Both President Bill Clinton and President George W. Bush have singled out the achievements of Wilma Rudolph for great praise. There have been many great athletes, but her unique position testifies not only to her athletic excellence, but to her dedication in using her celebrity to help others.

Wilma Rudolph herself provided the most fitting epitaph of all. "My great moment, if I left the earth today, would be knowing that I have tried to give something to young people."[10]

CHRONOLOGY

1940—Wilma Glodean Rudolph is born June 23 in St. Bethlehem, Tennessee.

1944—Contracts crippling polio.

1947—Enters Cobb Elementary School in Clarksville, Tennessee.

1952—Is able to walk without a brace; enters Burt High School for seventh grade.

1956—Wins bronze medal for the 400-meter relay race in Olympic games in Melbourne, Australia.

1958—Daughter Yolanda is born; joins the elite Tigerbelle women's track team at Tennessee A & I State University.

1960—Wins three Olympic gold medals: for the 100-meter dash, 200-meter dash, and 400-meter relay at the Olympic Games in Rome, Italy.

1961—Wins AAU James E. Sullivan Award as outstanding amateur.

1963—Graduates from Tennessee A & I State University; marries Robert Eldridge.

1964—Daughter Djuana is born.

1965—Son Robert Jr. is born.

1971—Son Xurry is born.

1977—Writes autobiographical book, *Wilma: The Story of Wilma Rudolph,* which is made into television motion picture.

1982—Establishes the Wilma Rudolph Foundation.

1992—Joins the Walking for Wellness project of the Black Women's Health Project.

1993—Chosen as one of the first five Americans to be awarded a National Sports Award in Washington, D.C.

1994—Dies on November 12 in Brentwood, Tennessee.

CHAPTER NOTES

Chapter 1. The Feeling of Freedom

1. Kristen Golden and Barbara Findlen, eds., *Remarkable Women of the Twentieth Century* (New York: Friedman/Fairfax Publishers, 1998), p. 20.

2. Wilma Rudolph, *Wilma: The Story of Wilma Rudolph* (New York: New American Library, 1977), p. 96.

3. Ibid., p. 98.

4. "Ahead of Their Time," *Runners World*, vol. 28, no. 6, June 1993.

Chapter 2. Childhood Struggle

1. Wilma Rudolph, *Wilma: The Story of Wilma Rudolph* (New York: New American Library, 1977), p. 36.

2. Ibid., p. 12.

3. Ibid., p. 36.

4. Ibid.

5. Ibid., p. 8.

6. Ibid., p. 18.

7. Kristen Golden and Barbara Findlen, eds., *Remarkable Women of the Twentieth Century* (New York: Friedman/Fairfax, 1998), p. 20.

8. Rudolph, p. 30.

9. Susan Reed, "Born to Win," *People Weekly*, November 28, 1994, p. 62.

10. Rudolph, p. 29.

11. Alexander Wolff and Richard O'Brien, "A Sprinter's Worth Is Measured Out in 10th of a Second," *Sports Illustrated*, November 21, 1994, p. 13.

12. *Encyclopedia of World Biography*, 2nd edition, vol. 17 (Detroit, Mich.: Gale Research, 1998), Biography Resource Center, Farmington Hills, Mich., Document K1631005718, p. 2.

13. Rudolph, p. 35.

14. *Contemporary Black Biography*, vol. 4 (Detroit, Mich.: Gale Research, 1998), Biography Resource Center, Farmington Hills, Mich., Document K1606001176, p. 2.

15. Deborah Gillan Straub, *Contemporary Heroes and Heroines*, Book II (Detroit, Mich.: Gale Research, 1992), Biography Resource Center, Farmington Hills, Mich., Document K1607000231, p. 2.

16. Ibid.

17. Rudolph, p. 19.

18. Ibid., p. 5.

19. Jessie Carnie Smith, ed., *Notable Black American Women*, Book I (Detroit, Mich.: Gale Research, 1992), Biography Resource Center, Farmington Hills, Mich., Document K1623000379, p. 2.

20. Ibid.

21. Ibid.

22. Rudolph, p. 24.

23. *Great Women in Sports* (Detroit, Mich.: Gale Research, 2002), Biography Resource Center, Farmington Hills, Mich., Document K1615000112, p. 2.

Chapter 3. A Star Athlete Is Born

1. Jessie Carnie Smith, ed., *Notable Black American Women*, Book I (Detroit, Mich.: Gale Research, 1992), Biography Resource Center, Farmington Hills, Mich., Document K1623000379, p. 12.

2. Ibid.

3. Ibid.

4. Wilma Rudolph, *Wilma: The Story of Wilma Rudolph* (New York: New American Library, 1977), p. 58.

5. Ibid.

6. Noah Adams, "Former Coach Pays Tribute to Wilma Rudolph," National Public Radio, *All Things Considered*, broadcast April 17, 1994.

7. Deborah Kent and Kathryn A. Quinlan, *Extraordinary People with Disabilities* (New York: Grolier Publishing, 1996), p. 140.

8. Rudolph, p. 63.

9. *Notable Black American Women*, p. 3.

10. Rudolph, p. 65.

11. Ibid., p. 76.

12. Ibid., p. 79.

13. Ibid.

Chapter 4. The Tigerbelle

1. *Encyclopedia of World Biography*, 2nd edition, vol. 17 (Detroit, Mich.: Gale Research, 1998), Biography Resource Center, Farmington Hills, Mich., Document K1631005718, p. 2.

2. Ibid.

3. Wilma Rudolph, *Wilma: The Story of Wilma Rudolph* (New York: New American Library, 1977), p. 108.

4. Ibid.

5. Ibid., p. 111.

6. Ibid.

7. Deborah Gillan Straub, *Contemporary Heroes and Heroines*, Book II (Detroit, Mich.: Gale Research, 1992), Biography Resource Center, Farmington Hills, Mich., Document K16070000231, p. 2.

8. Edna Rust and Art Rust, Jr., *Art Rust's Illustrated History of the Black Athlete* (New York: Doubleday Co., Inc., 1985), p. 3.

Chapter 5. Rome—1960

1. Bill Henry, *An Approved History of the Olympic Games* (Los Angeles: Southern California Committee for Olympic Games, 1981), p. 279.

2. Wilma Rudolph, *Wilma: The Story of Wilma Rudolph* (New York: New American Library, 1977), p. 127.

3. Ibid.

4. "Ahead of Their Time," *Runners World*, June 1993.

5. Ibid.

6. Jessie Carnie Smith, ed., *Notable Black American Women*, Book I (Detroit, Mich.: Gale Research, 1992), Biography Resource Center, Farmington Hills, Mich., Document K1623000379, p. 2.

7. Ibid.

8. Deborah Gillan Straub, ed., *Contemporary Heroes and Heroines*, Book II (Detroit, Mich.: Gale Research, 1992), Biography Resource Center, Farmington Hills, Mich., Document K1607000231, p. 1.

9. Rudolph, p. 136.

10. Noah Adams, "Former Coach Pays Tribute to Wilma Rudolph," National Public Radio, *All Things Considered*, broadcast April 17, 1994.

11. Ibid.

12. Ibid.

Chapter 6. Olympic Afterglow

1. Wilma Rudolph, *Wilma: The Story of Wilma Rudolph* (New York: New American Library, 1977), p. 137.

2. M. B. Roberts, "Rudolph Ran and the World Went Wild," ESPN, *Sports Center*, October 15, 2002, p. 3.

3. Jessie Carnie Smith, ed., *Notable Black American Women*, Book I (Detroit, Michigan: Gale Research, 1992), Biography Resource Center, Farmington Hills, Michigan, Document K1623000379, p. 4.

4. "Kilpatrick Introduces Bill to Award Congressional Medal to Wilma Rudolph," Webwire, Capitol Hill Press Release, October 23, 1997.

5. Rudolph, p. 145.

6. Ibid., p. 150.

7. Noah Adams, "Former Coach Pays Tribute to Wilma Rudolph," National Public Radio, *All Things Considered*, broadcast April 17, 1994.

8. William Nack, "Bonus Piece: As a Kid in Louisville the City Seemed So Big To Me," *Sports Illustrated*, January 13, 1992, p. 1.

9. Ibid.

10. Ibid.

11. Ibid.

12. Ibid.

13. *Encyclopedia of World Biography*, 2nd edition, vol. 17 (Detroit, Mich.: Gale Research, 1998), Biography Resource Center, Farmington Hills, Mich., Document K1631003718, p. 3.

Chapter 7. Retirement and Marriage

1. Wilma Rudolph, *Wilma: The Story of Wilma Rudolph* (New York: New American Library, 1977), p. 153.

2. Ibid., p. 145.

3. Deborah Gillan Straub, ed., *Contemporary Heroes and Heroines*, Book III (Detroit, Mich.: Gale Research, 1992),

Biography Resource Center, Farmington Hills, Mich., Document K160700231, p. 3.

4. Edna Rust and Art Rust, Jr., *Art Rust's Illustrated History of the Black Athlete* (New York: Doubleday & Co., 1985), p. 353.

5. Bobby L. Lovett, "Leaders of Afro-American Nashville," Nashville Conference on Afro-American Culture and History Newsletter, 1997.

Chapter 8. Career and Motherhood

1. Wilma Rudolph, *Wilma: The Story of Wilma Rudolph* (New York: New American Library, 1977), p. 158.

2. "Memorandum to the Vice President in Response to His Report on the Summer Youth Opportunity Campaign," August 15, 1966, p. 825.

3. Alexander Wolff and Richard O'Brien, "A Sprinter's Worth Is Measured Out in 10th of a Second," *Sports Illustrated*, November 21, 1994, p. 13.

4. Rudolph, p. 161.

5. Ibid., p. 162.

6. Ibid.

7. Jessie Carnie Smith, ed., *Notable Black American Women*, Book I (Detroit, Mich.: Gale Research, 1992), Biography Resource Center, Farmington Hills, Mich., Document K1623000379, p. 2.

8. Rudolph, p. 162.

9. Bobby L. Lovett, "Leaders of Afro-American Nashville," Nashville Conference on Afro-American Culture and History Newsletter, 1997.

Chapter 9. The Foundation and the Last Walk

1. Deborah Gillan Straub, ed., *Contemporary Heroes and Heroines*, Book III (Detroit, Mich.: Gale Research, 1992),

Biography Resource Center, Farmington Hills, Mich., Document K160700231, p. 2.

2. Kristen Golden and Barbara Findlen, eds., *Remarkable Women of the Twentieth Century* (New York: Friedman/Fairfax Publishers, 1998), p. 20.

3. Susan Reed, "Born to Win," *People Weekly*, November 28, 1994, p. 62.

4. M. B. Roberts, "Rudolph Ran and the World Went Wild," ESPN, *Sports Center*, October 15, 2002, p. 3.

5. "When the Sun Shines," *Daily Celebrations 2000*, October 24, 1999, p. 1.

6. *Great Women in Sports* (Detroit, Mich.: Gale Research, 2002), Biography Resource Center, Farmington Hills, Mich., Document K1615000112, p. 3.

7. Kevin L. Carter, "Determination Is Key, Olympian Tells Women," *Los Angeles Times*, April 16, 1986, p. 2.

8. Ibid.

9. Ibid.

10. Dick Russell, *Black Genius* (New York: Carroll & Graf, 1998), p. 401.

11. *Newsmakers*, issue 4 (Detroit, Mich.: Gale Research, 1995).

12. Ibid.

13. Noah Adams, "Former Coach Pays Tribute to Wilma Rudolph," National Public Radio, *All Things Considered*, broadcast April 17, 1994.

14. "A Celebration of Wilma," Tennessee State University press release, November 17, 1994, p. 2.

Chapter 10. The Legacy of a Champion

1. Randy Harvey, "Olympic Legend Wilma Rudolph Dies," *Los Angeles Times*, November 13, 1994, p. A-1.

2. "Florence Joyner Pays Tribute to the Late Wilma Rudolph," *Jet*, December 12, 1994, p. 51.

3. James A. Page, *Black Olympian Medalists* (Edgewood, Colo.: Libraries Unlimited, 1991), p. 15.

4. Athelia Knight, "Olympic Track Star Wilma Rudolph Dies," *The Washington Post*, November 13, 1994, p. D5.

5. "Governor Proclaims June 23 as Wilma Rudolph Day," Tennessee News Release, June 20, 1997.

6. Dick Russell, *Black Genius* (New York: Carroll & Graf Publishers, 1998), p. 40.

7. "Kilpatrick Introduces Bill to Award Congressional Medal to Wilma Rudolph," Webwire, Capitol Hill Press Release, October 23, 1997.

8. Ibid.

9. "The Police Athletic League's Wilma Rudolph Track Club Starts Its 2001 Season," Media Release, March 30, 2001.

10. *Encyclopedia of World Biography*, 2nd edition, vol. 17 (Detroit, Mich.: Gale Research, 1998), Biography Resource Center, Farmington Hills, Mich., Document K1631003718, p. 3.

FURTHER READING

Coffee, Wayne. *Wilma Rudolph: Beating the Odds.* Detroit, Mich.: Gale Group, 1992.

Ditchfield, Christin. *Top 10 Olympic Gold Medalists.* Berkeley Heights, N.J.: Enslow Publishers, Inc., 2000.

Manley, Claudia B. *Competitive Track and Field.* New York: Rosen, 2001.

Rudolph, Wilma. *Wilma: The Story of Wilma Rudolph.* New York: New American Library, 1977. (This is Rudolph's autobiography.)

Ruth, Amy. *Wilma Rudolph.* Minneapolis, Minn.: Lerner, 2000.

Sherrow, Victoria. *Wilma Rudolph: Champion Athlete.* Broomall, Pa.: Chelsea House, 1995.

INTERNET ADDRESSES

"Wilma Rudolph"
<http://www.galegroup.com/free_resources/bhm/bio/rudolph_w.htm>

M. B. Roberts. "Rudolph Ran and the World Went Wild."
<http://espn.go.com/sportscentury/features/00016444.html>

"Wilma Rudolph: Overcoming Childhood Handicaps"
<http://www.olympic.org/uk/athletes/heroes/bio_uk.asp?PAR_I_ID=10427>

INDEX

Pages with photographs are in boldface type.